SHEBAH

RISING IN THE JUDGEMENT

Poems By Shebah Ali

Publish by The Gathering of the People Publishing

Cover design by Shebah Ali

Copyright Shebah Ali

Published and printed in the USA

Ras Tafari

Reign on Earth

The Queen of the South will rise at the judgment with this generation and condemn it; for she came from the ends of the earth to listen to Solomon's wisdom, and now something greater than Solomon is here.

...Mathew 12:42

As a people we must come together on one common ground there is an Almighty Ruler. Who is Sovereign and above all things? Jehovah is most high and lifted up. We must believe that through the Almighty all things belong to us. We must ask Abba the father to open our ears so that we may hear his voice. Because of rebellion our ears have been shut. We must humble ourselves and turn from our ungodly ways. Its then when we seek his face that he will hear our cries. We must ask for forgiveness and direction. Obedience to the creator deems us worthy. The creator has chosen you amongst all people to be special to him to rule. You can change the atmosphere.

History

JAH THE GIVER AND TAKER OF LIFE

HAS BESTOWED UPON ME

THE GIFT OF ICE

TO DRIP THE JEWELS THEREOF

JEWELS OF LOVE

I come from a black history

I am a black mystery

I am the half

That has never been told

Now I come to unfold

My story

So full of glory

It's about a queen

Who had bling

And anything else

She dreamed

She heard about a king

Doing his thing

Across the land

She had to fulfill the plan

She has to see with her own eyes

The one they say was so wise

She loved that man

As soon as she laid eyes on him

She knew he was a gem

She stayed there for quite a while

When she left she was with child

She had that precious seed

She took it back

(To preserve the black)

Oh what a joy

She had a baby boy

When her son was 17+1

She went back across the land

So her kid could see his old man

They stayed there for sometime

When they left

They left with shine

His father was a king

So he didn't just give him anything

He got laced

With a portion of his race

The scepter kingly rod blessed by God

His fathers throne he took home

The A of C.

(Ark of the Covenant)

Was moved because of prophecy

When the king was no more

And the people were scattered

All that was battered

Did not Matter

(The seed was preserved)

It kept glowing it kept growing

It's not a trick the boy was Menelik

Now it's not a mystery My STORY

It's history HIS STORY

The scepter shall not depart from Judah, nor a lawgiver from between his feet, until Shiloh come; and unto him *shall* the gathering of the people *be*.

ISRAEL

YOU DON'T KNOW WHO YOU ARE

OK LOOK STAR

It started from a promise

To a man name Abraham

Who was willing to sacrifice his own son

That's how he got to be the chosen one

Yes he was then blessed

The multiplying of his seeds

Would not rest

They would be as the stars of heaven

And the sand, which is upon the sea

We're part of that blessing

You and me

Oh you don't know who you are

Poppy you're a star

Oh you don't know who you are

Mommy you're a star

By choice Abraham

Obeyed JAH voice

Now this is the Wake up

His grandson Jacob

Who God named Israel

He started the trail

Hear the deal

Feel the vibe

He had 12 sons

Which grew into12 tribes

They lived as slaves in Egypt

Because of a slip

10 envied 1 brother

Jealousy made them all suffer

They multiplied as it was written

Moses was born and it was on

All Males 2 and under

Should be smitten

Oh you don't know who you are

Son you're a star

Oh you don't know who you are

Baby girl you're a star

Moses was saved

With the help of JAH

The Israelites

Were no longer slaves

After all we went through

We had only one thing to do

That was to follow the rule

We had a covenant that protected us

We had a ruler who respected us

Put him behind, that's why we don't shine

Now you know who you are

ISRAEL YOU'RE STARS

Israel for us today

That in blessing I will bless thee, and in multiplying I will multiply thy seed as the stars of the heaven, and as the sand, which is upon the seashore; and thy seed shall possess the gate of his enemies;

...Genesis 22:17

You are being deployed

To live a lifestyle of faith

STRIVING

We will strive to bring about the tribes

Things in our scribes our notes

Although we came on boats

Ships packed with hate as we debate

If we have enough on our plates

We are still are hungry

For the knowledge

Of the father our savior

New lessons are going to be taught

Our history will be sought

We will get in the books

To take a look

At places and times

That are in our minds

Things so vivid

That our hearts see so clear

It is here this is the year

When the lord

Will take all who are bored

And teach them

Let's reach them

Rakim Allah

He moved the crowd

With the magic he posses

The God is blessed

Me as an earth

The right rules

Be there or be square

Our cypher will be tight

Wrap with the might

From the one

With the ultimate gun

JAH

The ruler

The creator

We are all reborn in this storm

To bring about the calm

That is to come

The peace not made by the beast

But by the man

With the ultimate plan

The plan of life

We will take what we know

And show your brothers and sisters

Mothers and fathers

That we will hit the hardest

Knowledge

Being kicked by a goddess

A pretty black queen

Who was taught to wear jeans

But posses what is so mean

To bring them green dollars and cents

To all ladies and gents

We are about to make it happen

Start snapping

Feel the vibe

From a sister

From a tribe of Israel

Being broke down in the fullest

Pull us down and

Watch us stand tall

To preach to all

Good and bad

About what we had

How we were Kings and Queens

Who gleamed

in the presence of the sun

We were one

And will always be

You and me

We are special

We are a chosen people

From a chosen place

That they tried to hide erase

A place far across the sea

That's where we should be

In the land of love

That came from above

Not beyond

We are going

To get back all that is ours

We will be showered

With love

The God know it

He has been trying to show it

But you weren't ready

To be rocked steady

With the beat

From the Congo the drums

Look at my black queens

Look at them in their glory

Telling history to all mankind

For all man good

From hoods

To cities to states

It's going to be great

Oh what a sight to behold

Dripping jewels of gold

Shebah

The half that has never been told

Wait

Let patience have its perfect way

Rome was not built in a day

The road may seem endless

May even be rocky

Keep moving never give up

On your dreams

We are always climbing ascending in life

With strife and stride

We succeed if only we believe

Lets be inspired

To strictly desire

The one who is higher

Stolen

Acura Ghana

That's why you have to have it Tawana

Off the coast you were stole

So was your gold

That's why to hold and control

Fine jewelry its no mystery

We want what belongs to us

Go ahead lust

Before the dreaded years of tears

Before the careless fearless

Ones with the guns

Before the name change

And the lightening of the skin

Before the cotton fields

You were Israel

Before the rape of woman and culture

We structured magnificent pyramids

The sphinx think

Timbuktu is you

From whips to chips micro sized

From erased to hide

From despised to disowned

This is the call from home

I want all Africans to stand

Be accounted for

War is ahead

Don't fear the dead

It is the living

That is giving power to the wicked

What about you

I'm sick of it

Hard body

By the grace of God

I'm going hard

Rooted then suited up

To sup with the Royals

A Loyal Solider

Solid

God has got this Miss

On a Mission

Because crucifixion

Is becoming a fad

Tattooed on body parts

But not in the hearts

Souls that are dying

He hears the crying

Rise Up to Wise Up

Oh ye Wandering Souls

Goals cans be reached

So I'll teach

Thru rhyme until that time

When Shiloh Comes

Until we hear the drums

The trumpets and the harps

Until the Arch Angels

Dismantles the Enemy's plan

Yeshua sits at the Right Hand

IN COMMAND OF OUR DESTINY,

IN DEMAND OF OUR TESTIMONIES

Escape the ordinarily

You are Earths rightful rulers

Because of your clothes

You were sold

Took your gold

Stole your soul

Rewrote history

And tell it how they want it told

Aint that bold

They call us cold

Every other man on probation or parole

If you weak you fold

If you strong make a mold

Seeds of your likeness

What it is to be righteous

Despite this mess

You are blessed

Praying

I'm praying that it wont be long

Before we are strong

And can right any wrong

Hopeful is my song

I'll sing till I'm gonged

Off the show

I will never let go

Of the feelings inside

I will never try to hide

I will never let go

I'll help us to grow

I'm glad the cements is not dry

So we can give this another try

Let's take the good

From our foundation

Stir in some patients

We might ...just be all right

Born

My wait is timeless

The love is infinite

With this gift

I want to shower you

Keep you safe

From those who wish to devour you

I want to strong tower you

Who was I made for

Black and sexy

Some vex me

Some scorn

The day I was born

The 70's was heavenly

The earth received

A gift of prestige

Shooting Stars

Everything from the hood

Will be made good

My niggers

Won't pull triggers

They will reload

With the gold bullets

Shooting out knowledge

Far like the stars

That's what we are

Stars

We all shine in time

We will all take our place

In this race

So that when we see his face

We will be ready

To rock the people steady

Straight is the path

Who know math

Add it up 1+1 has always been 2

Now I know what I have to do

I will clean this mess

Clear the eyes

I learned from the wise

No one will despise

All eyes will be opened

You're yearning

For the learning

For the teachings

The doctrines will be revealed

To heal all my people

Those who are sick of it

From the wicked

I'm not here to change

Just rearrange

Hearts Souls Mind

To awake the blind

From the

Diaspora

I call ya

With lessons

That are blessings

I come to stop to

Yield all

To call

My peoples in the field

Doing what had to be done

So that we could be one …again

My people it is time

I'm doing it with rhyme

Everyone will know

How **history** go

From Adam to eve

To Paula and Steve

From Rashod

Will come God

Jah is not in the sky

Look up

But not for him

But for them

So they can see

What was and will always be

That's Black

The beauty it holds

It's hot like coal

Were coming back in our glory

To tell History

The way it should be told

To the young & to the old

To the world

All boys and girls

Will hear his name forevermore

Before I walk through the door

The teaching

The preaching

The lessons

Will be blessings

Be prepared for the real storm

You don't need coats

Cause it will be warm

Burning hot

Lets not stop

Till we take this straight

To the top

We will bring the enemy down

Myth or Gift

Babies having babies

Is it a myth or a gift

They say that's crazy

Multiply let those seeds loose

If you have don't have a clue

Just stay in school

Do the knowledge

That's your tool for life

Whether you're a

Princess- Queen or wife

Education is a must

So while you lust

After bigger busts or butts

Just have the guts

Take time to elevate the mind

It's your jewel

It sits on the top

Encrowning a body of splendor

To any encounter

No matter the gender

Don't be a pretender

Make it happen

For you and your seeds

Please the needs

Of the youth

Watch like a possum

The blossom of life

That you bring

From swing to cars

Watch your stars

Soar not sour

Jah is Real

Jah is Love

Oh what a sight to be hold

The Half That Has Never Been Told

He put it in my hand

To clear the plan

To make the way for his day

If you don't know how

I will show you the bow

Get on your knees

Say please

ABBA forgive me

For the wrong that I have done

I wanted to have fun

But tonight

I want to make it right

Not fight

I want to embrace your light

Cause your love give me feelings

That I can't explain

I don't want to

I just want to shout your name

JAH

Halleujah

In my lifetime

I need to see a whole lot of love,

In my lifetime the love that is old

Will be made forever young

Queen

Oh what a sight to behold

The Half That Has Never Been Told

You can't stop the reign

The kingdom has come

And if you don't know

It's time for freedom

I'm a Queen not Elizabeth

The one who brings forth briquettes

From across the river Nile

The blessed and holy soil

Dark and Lovely

Black and comely

I am blessed with the knowledge

From the highest of colleges

The might of the Trinity

All wrapped in Divinity

I come with fierceness

Of a lioness

Not to mention

The greatness I posses

I bring Distress

To all those who oppress

The people

Of his royal highness

430 years is enough

Its time to settle the score

Come on Let the Lions Roar

From David to Solomon

Menelik to King Selassie I

The lion had prevailed

To open the seal

Don't be surprised

It's not just how way I feel

It's from the books

That you teach

That this prophesy is revealed

What a sight to behold

Speaking of the half

That never even told

Shebah

You can't stop the reign

The kingdom has come

And if you don't know

It's time for freedom

RED-GOLD-GREEN

I BE THAT QUEEN

WITH LONG

BUT NOT LOST DREAMS

Nightmares

About to be become reality

You see

Through my third eye

Light is being shed

For the dead

Who walk and sleep

Who creep in jeeps

Navigate the state

That your people are in

From birth to death

They want us left

Sleepwalkers Sharp talkers

Players balling hear the calling

From the Queen

I be She

Bye Bye

If you're not ready to ride

The new V

The ultimate device

For the times to come

From the slums

To plush sofas

I'm calling all loafers

Make your quota

In the mind game

Diamonds are ours

Gifts from Yeshua

No who you are

Be that star

Israel

The Valleys are still wet

From tears and sweat

Interruptions of daily life styles

Many miles

Crowns wait

Many in this state

The royal family

With the A of C

(Ark of the Covenant)

Buried

Deep in memory

Never to be forgotten

Only reveal to heal

and

I be that queen

With long but not lost dreams

My banner

RED GOLD & GREEN

Where my sinners @

now I know

where my winners @

Let's be changed

In his name

Turn your heart towards the Almighty

For as sure as the sun sets in the west

Grace keeps us blessed

The shower of his excellence

In his existence there's no comparison

STARTING OVER

MY DREAMS TODAY

TO SHOW A BETTER WAY

START BELIEVING IN YOURSELF

YOU WILL HAVE MORE THAN WEALTH

YOU ARE THE BEST THING

EVER MADE REGARDLESS

OF YOUR SHADE

LET'S KNOCKDOWN

ON THE LOCKDOWNS

LET'S CLOCK NOW

HOW TO FLOCK DOWN

ON THEM

SWARM THEM

WITH THE RIGHTOUSNESS

DESPITE THIS MESS

WE ARE IN

START TEACHING THE RIGHT

STOP TRYING TO FIGHT

STOP THE PATTERNS

STOP REPEATING

DISCOVER NEW TREATMENTS

GO ON WITH THE PROCEEDINGS

STOP THE GRIEVING

I UNDERSTAND

THAT YOU HAVE TO BE PROTECTED

CAUSE YOU FEEL NEGLECTED

BUT YOU ARE LOVED

NOT REJECTED

IT'S IN YOUR MIND

STOP TRYING TO FIND

PEACE EATING UP THE STREETS

BRING DOWN THE HEAT

THEN COMPLAIN

HOW THEY CALL YOUR NAME

YOU'RE MAKING YOUR FAME

THEY KNOW YOU

BECAUSE OF WHAT YOU DO

YOU GOT A HISTORY

TO START FROM

NOT THE NIGGER

GETTING THE ONES

IN LUMP SUMS

FROM THE GUNS

TAKING YOUR MAN

FOR A GRAND

MESSING UP THE BIGGER PLAN

WE NEED You'll SOLDIERS

TO HOLD US DOWN

IT'S A ROCKY ROAD

THAT'S WHAT I'M TOLD

WHAT'S THE SOURCE

OF YOUR PAIN

TRYING TO REIGN

LOOK KING DO YOUR THING

AUNT SISTA NIECE

TRYING TO GIVE YOU A PIECE

OF HOW I FEEL

WITH YOUR SO CALLED

INSTINCT TO KILL

WE ALREADY LOST...MILL...

HOW MANY MORE TO STEEL

God is REAL

GOD IS LOVE

GOD IS HERE

Real warriors

I'm drafting real warriors

No comic book stories here

Batman scat man

Cleopatra is getting at ya

Begin with the red

Cause the dead speak

Teach they say

Educate elevate stimulate

Motivate most of all captivate

The mind

Diamonds the stones

That are buried and grown

First the live gems Israel

Has to be united

To long divide

Misled uniformed

In the wrong uniform

Soldiers in the wrong army

Spiderman was grand

But David slew goliath

No myth our gift

Pete been that rock

Now we laying down

A new foundation

For the nations are rising

No more dividing

We adding up multiplying

Love has given

Us another chance

To finish the plan

To be the humans

It was fortold

You get the gold

Go shine Go shine Go shine

It's not to late

A pressing for a migration

Separation for the preparation

Prepare for the beating

And the blessings

through lessons

We were taught

You were bought

You have your ticket

Away from the wicked

Got get it!

Seeds

It's disastrous were they're taking it

Forget the budget

Get briquettes diamonds

For the mines are ours

Gifts from YESHUA

Trust we lust our own antiquities

Let's speak to the seeds

Behold the beauty

Iesha –Tameka Taminika

We are blessed

Bonafied structures of magic

It's no trick

Slick chicks

With gifts to gab grab

Hold, mold and control

It's coming

Hear the humming birds

Flying like bats out of hell

Baby-girls rising

Can't be stopped do your thing

Bring the angels back

Watch it come

The beauty in BLACK

Rider

I soaked it all up in silence

Trying to be like king

Non-violent

With pride is my stride

To get me where I needed to be

But I did not need a V

Just the gas

The energy to be who I be

A Black Queen

With the colors

Red gold & green

I was dripped with Red Blood of love

That was pumped in my veins

Be before I got my name

Shining with a gold

That was so bold

Yet so bright

That special light

Guiding me

To a safe place

My black race

The green was the land

From which the plan

Did start

To keep the beat in my heart

Of the Congo drums

One by one

We hit it

Now is the time to get it

The ones

Not the guns

To build from the crumbs

They left us

I get confused

With the words in green

They want us to think it's for the cream

But it's not

It's for is the Land

That is grand

Very big across many seas

A lot of waters

That's where we're we came from

Sons and daughters

Across the waters

Sacred Prostitution

Oh yes I'm blessed

With Divine Energy

Covered by Flesh

I keep the god hard

Spinning 360 degrees

On his knees

Straight begging please

Sexual Ecstasy

I'm more than just a V

For you to ride

Than slide to the next one

Trying to have fun

Sacred prostitution

Is not the resolution?

Its crucifixion

Starts switching

Up your style

Change it for while

I laugh in delight

At the sight

Of you at night

Trying to get at my tight

When you can differentiate

The feminine components

Not just what to bone it

See beyond my physical

Feel me mystical

I taste ice sickles

Not testicles

So if you BALLIN

Mind you fall into

My black hole that controls

A part of the soul

On the other side of wrath

Is grace

You want a taste

It might be bitter

It might be sweet

Guaranteed to meet

Your maker

I'll take ya

There so beware

It's all in there

DECISIONS

VALLEY OF DECISION

HE WILL HAVE THEM IN DERICION

BECAUSE OF THE PRISIONS

WHERE THE SOULS ARE DWELLING

WE HEAR THE YELLING

FOR MORE TO BE BUILT

TO BE FILLED WITH FILTH

THAT THEY RELATE TO OUR RACE

AS WE BLINDLY FILL UP THE SPACE

I'M HOLLERING WAIT

STOP THE NON SENSE

BEING CONVICTS

SLAVES TO THE SYSTEM

YOU CAN'T RESIST THEM

FIND THE SIMPLEST THING TO DO

YOU CHOOSE IT

DON'T LET IT CHOOSE YOU

LIFE IS A BIG ROAD

WITH A LOT OF SIGNS

OPEN THE MIND

USE WHAT YOU GOT

FILL YOUR OWN SLOT

WITH A SLUG

NOT FROM A SO CALLED THUG

TRYING TO GET PROPS

ON A BLOCK THAT IS ALREADY HOT

WE ARE ALL VICTUMS

EVEN THE SLICK ONES

THEY TRICK'EM TOO

KEEP IT TIGHT

WITH THE RIGHT

AND YOU CANT GO WRONG

WHAT IS STRONG IS STRONG

YOURE LIKE STEEL (ISRAEL)

YOU CAN GET THROUGH IT

YOU CAN GET OVER IT

SO SEW IT

LOCK IT DOWN

IN YOUR TOWN

(YOUR STATE OF MIND)

YOU CAN RESIST THEM

Knowledge Wisdom & Understanding

Is what *I am* Demanding

Storms

Like nuclear power

My words devour

Beware of the chain reaction

Fasten your seat belt

Obey the laws of his daughter

Deeper than water

No waste no spills

I release spells

Souls bound to hell

Geophysics

I survey the area

Digging up mess instantly

Like a tornado

Witness me

Severe thunderstorm

Far more average from the norm

Casualties –fatalities –natural disasters

Sticking the game like plaster

Seeking out our masters

SKYS DARKEN when I reign

Hearken the Queen

In MY Presence

Only the essence

The one's with the blessings

Will escape my lightning bolts

More than 6,000 volts

Making Fake hair stand

While, I devise future plans

To conquer the land

No Son of Sam

Of daughter of Shaytan

Just a righteous woman

Out of control

Taking souls

Cause the Flesh is weak

Hear the speech

Dearly beloved

We are gathered

To bear witness to the rising of

Shebah

In the judgment

To condemn the prudent

From the uttermost

Parts of the earth

They will be searched

All praises due

She is for you

Shebah

Where the herbs and the spices

Are the nicest

The streets are paved with gold

Let it be told

The motherland

Is older than

Any ancestor

Where the remains still stain the rocks

The clock stop

Time stood still

Israel in the hills

The valleys cry

Never saying goodbye

Stolen and scattered

Still to be battered

Let me go back to the stones

Where my bones

Are crushed

Because you rushed

Your greatness over my back

Oh how you wacked with your whip

To get me on your ship

To sail where I don't know or want to go

Shebah

Where the herb and the spices

Are the nicest

The streets are paved with gold

Let it be told

The motherland

Is older than

Any ancestor

Why did you bring me here

To embed a fear

To keep me scared

Of my own kind

Give me my mind

Cause its mine

From long time

I was the only one

Under the sun

It rose on me

I grew to see beauty

In my eyes was put wise

You want me to despise

Could never be

Cause I know me

Could never take away

What is here

Is meant to stay

The rest forget

I'm in a mess

But I won't stress

Cause I know I'm blessed

I'll take heed to my seed

It's in my deed

I know my landlord

I sewed this for him

I plowed his garden

To harden the burdens

That was to be made

As many was slayed

I prayed to keep the roots

Where they belong

The only way to stay strong

We know we did wrong

Cause we still do

Our hearts are weary

More than weak

So we speak

In all tongues

To the old

And to the young

To get back our glory

We have to tell HISTORY

SINFUL

DEPRAVED WICKED

I'm sick of it

Vote for Jah

Shout Halleujah

Cast your ballet

Validate your faith

Don't wait the seventh

Think about Heaven

Let pray like never before

Open the door

Let's even the score

I want to hear the Lion and Lioness

ROOOOOOOOOOAR!!!!

A nation living in hell

Whether sick or well

It's all the same

Greater than any name

I AM in the Game

Youth in Asia

I praise ya

On the streets

From the womb

Don't think about

Being a groom

The words are too sad

But your is father mine too

We share the same message in the Life

Our brother Christ

I'm wrap tight with the might

From all that is right

My light has shown

I have grown

Now I have to go on

Grow on you

Want a Story dripped with glory

Let me let you about Israel

This girl is out of control

You just can't hold this down

But you can be turned around

And hit in the face with your race

All eyes shift

On this empress

Rise up

The fist let'em rise

Keep your eyes on the prize

Do you despise

Or just disrespect

Because of neglect

No daddy

Sadly I feel your grief

Madly I hit the streets

Gladly I reach for the stars

Forgotten the bars

Healing the scars

Deep wounds soon to be erase

Traced myself

Spaced myself

Place myself

Front line warrior

On the battlefield

My armor righteousness

Test by the one who bless

Confessed his name

With no shame

Put in the game

To rearrange

Proper order

From a daughter

Glorify the **son**

Let's be one

Know the need

To feed

The youth

Renew my mind

So that I can find

All that my soul is searching for

Let me continue to store

Your word in my heart

Let us never part

My desire is to stand in your gates

Eat from faith filled plates

Keep your angles encamped around me

I want to be free

Feed me your manna

Nourish my soul today

Hosanna

Church

I'm an insert in the church

To inject

Well direct

The soul to resurrect

Wake up

Take up your bed

And the veil from your eyes

Arise in faith

Cast your bait

Flood gates being released

In the season, no treason

No prisoners, no visitors

Permanent residents

In the building

Cause we're yielding

To our call

From the all seeing

We are being lifted

Thru the gifted

And the anointed messages

We deliver, I quicken

When the voice says

Better days are here

Fear not

I am the Lord thy God

Who saved thee

Look for greater

Only Up on this elevator…

Who's listening

Diving positioning

Inspiriting a nation

To change their situation

Deprivation over

We're eating lovely

Drunk off

The bubbly of life

Strife is mandatory

It makes your story

Individual and unique

To help you complete

Your journey

And reach your destiny

To the best of me

I'm in this

For us to win this

HAPPY HOUR

When the children of the most high

Shout Hallelujah

Halle U Jah

No sickness No disease

All impurities release

Light conquering the world

Overcoming darkness

No more hardness

Jehovah

With your many names

In your presences

Shazam

We've been changed

When we come through the door

All at once

No shaking No mistaking

Only the placing of proper order

For all sons and daughters

Lets' sit down and reason

Because of treason

It's pleasing

To me to see

The gifted- lifted

Transitioned

Things have shifted

In the earthly realm

The gems polished

Kept safe

Now put in place

The veil has been torn

The 7th seal broken

Released by spoken word

Capturing before the

Rapturing of the sky

Unify unified

Through Spirit

Can you hear it

The silent trumpet

The shofah

Dancing like David

Hallelujah

We made it Aba is pleased

I am up cause the word has to be heard

A new caper for the paper

I didn't start this I am just apart of this

Culture Queens

We stay having dreams

To be in the limelight

Keep yourself tight

With right you can't go wrong

Be strong

Yall miss Diana Ross

I'm the new boss

Coming down soul train

Raining on your hard

Like Bruce Lee or Willis

Gorillas in the mist

Of the concrete jungle

Bundle up

Cause the codes are comings

Numbing all souls

Froze chilly for real

New world order

For sons and daughters

DEW

There's a lily

In the valley

Go and tell somebody

In the mist of corruption

Instructions are given

For righteous living

The golden rule

We must follow

For green pastures

Pastors Prophets

Evangelist Teachers

Continue to reach us

The surplus

Is enough

To serve

Style

Sistas dig your style

They would walk a mile

Just to be in your bed

Will you do your job

Put the knowledge in their head

Or the understanding between their legs

Giving him something he can feel

That's what she's all about

Getting all he can get

Sons turning her out

Making her give up her dreams

Now she is on his team

She never thought about leaving school

Only thought about being cool

She never thought life could be so cruel

Now labeled one of the fools

She is no longer a little girl

She's bringing one into the world

Now what am I going to do with this baby

You're going to raise her

To be a lady

But I never learned

Guess what now it's your turn

They say you reap what you sew

Now make it grow

Make it stay alive for more than 25

Don't let it leave your side

Don't let your babies stray

Keep the roots strong from day to day

And you will forever be shown the way

STOP LOOKING

JUST OPEN YOUR EYES

I am Queen Shebah

From the DEPTHS,

I have come

To straighten out this mess

To tell you

What you already know

We're blessed

We are Jewels

We've been shinning

Son-sun-star

Who ever you are

Shine wake up

Take your place

It's not to late

We are

Kings queens

Princes and princesses

From a long line of greatness

Not the mess

That they claim that we are

Stop picking up those guns

Stop running after the ones

Everything you need is right hear

In your head

In your heart

Make a start

Change Rearrange

Awake take

The veil off of your eyes

You are wise

The blessed seeds are us

Adeyinka

On fire for the messiah

It's long been my desire

To spit this-I mean witness

With a relentless passion

I'm smashing/casting

Down all vain thoughts

I've been bought

Been set free

Because of me he was bruised

How dare I cruise

Through life with a high head

Forgetting or not acknowledging

The blood that was shed

On Calvary

I got work to do

And so do you

For the sake of Zion I dare not be silent

Surrounded with crowns

Banging

I joined a gang/army

That brings harmony

A peace that surpasses all understanding

Commanding souls

to take hold of life

to live more abundantly

demanding all ungodly

to flee from within

come out

There is no space

or place for unrighteousness

we're marching stampeding

exceeding and exceling

all the while yelling

I'm soldier in the army of the LORD

Capturing clans of shaytans

Converting and inserting

The master's plan

Walk a path directed by God illuminated by faith

Enter In

In that secret place

I found space

I found time

I found my mind

My joy and my peace

Increased

When I entered in

I surrendered then

All that I had known

And all I was shown

Could not compare

To the atmosphere

in is presence

Oh the essence

of his being

Oh the unspoken glory

Surly

This is life

Keep your aspirations high

One step towards your goal

Is a piece to the puzzle

of your soul

in the face of defeat

stay with the one who is complete

you may not see it with the naked eye

there is a plan for your life

you're one of a kind

a brilliant mind

waiting to be released

You're in the master's hands

It's all in his plan

The ancient of days is grand

Peace love an harmony

Is the rhythm

One drum under the sun

One thing one string

Play his music

Use it don't abuse it

I am not hear to change

But to rearrange

The hearts the souls the mind

Awake the blind

Let them know

Jah is God

Jah is Real

Jah is Love

Jah is the everlasting light

Behind the clouds of mystery

History has to be told

It is so old

But yet new

To a few who have

And never knew

His name

Jah make the way

For the people today

To stop being stubborn

And learn the truth

For the youth

Will be the ones who see it

It's in our children to be it

The light will shine

And things will be made

As it should be.

One for all

Together we stand tall.

Hear and obey what I say

About Jah today

Listen take heed

Feed the need

Let the stories be told

Take heed not for greed

But for life Jah life

Oh what a sight to behold

Better than gold

What a sight to behold

We will shine in time we will shine

What a sight to behold

The truth is here to be told

You want glitter you want gold

You want truth to be told

Oh what a sight to behold.

My gifts are valueless

That heed to what I bring

My words I want to sting

As I do my thing

This is what I bring

Stories full of glory

I shout in the day and in the night

Cause this is a sight

Jah Light let it reign

Say it again let it reign

Jah is real harder than steel

His might is tight

Jah is here to rule

Forever in a day to come

I'll beat it in your head with the drum

The days have come we will shine

I will have what is mine

Jah gives us the glory to the history

Jah love is here to heal the nations

With fist of fury and love that is glory

Jah is real he is great our savior

Let his name be heard

By boys and girls across the world

Jah is real we sing his praise

In these days a better way is coming

That is what I'm humming.

Take your place in this race

Front line don't doubt mine

I got a story I want to tell it I want to yell

I vibe with Jam bet that

Well bet this it is a no miss

A hit and win situation

Is what I bring to this engagement

Marry me my knowledge stay in love

Don't miss out on what I'm saying

Cause I'm hitting harder than a bee sting

What I bring is joy

Just pure satisfaction to make it happen

Am I tripping or dripping

With knowledge of self

That's going to bring wealth

Oh what a sight to behold

Destiny

I am destined to reign

I am a Queen

I want my crown my throne

My castles to call home

Where my diamonds

Lions in this jungle

Cats meow meow

Been around 9 lives

I'm one of Solomon's wives

Menelik was my son

I am the one

The Half That Has Never Been Told

Rolling the scrolls releasing

Seals for ISRAEL

from Brownsville…

what a sight to behold

we shine better than any piece of gold

His knowledge is being bestowed upon me

so that I can teach

for the truth I seek

my people must take heed

cause the time is at hand

I am a black Queen not from queens

But from Brooklyn

Spike lee's Crooklyn

I am feeling a vibe

That came from a tribe

not quest but seeking the word yes

vibe with me to the mountaintop

where heads bop to the rhythm

The beats of the Congo drums

Abound in hope

By the power of the spirit be groped

Watching

I gladly see

Prophesy being fulfilled

Through real time

I madly speak to mine cause at hand

Is the master's plan

Calling out

And poring out

Spirits

Can you hear it

The drum line is forming

Storming the fields

For all of Israel

I fadly reach

Through social networks

I teach

Follow me on twitter @shebahali

Facebook Shebah Irie

Lift up burdens

Your loins girded

You righteous servants

You I choose

You I choose

Not to lose

I'll hold on tight

I know it's right

Not even in my dreams

Have I seen one so Angelic

Let me relic the moment forever

You and I together

Happiness is with you

Lord show me what to do

So I can be pleasing

Let us reason

Can we grow and walk side by side

In faith we can glide

Soar the heaven Kiss the stars

Visit the Milky Way and pass by mars

To infinity and beyond

Just sit by the pond

Throw some rocks

I want us to dark in many docks

Spreading kindness going spineless

Adventures let's venture to the future

Sweet paths

Lord it is only you I yearn for

My knocking is at your door

I will seek until I find

I will have what is mine

With you in mind

All the while

Through all the trials and tribulations

I will still without hesitation

Rejoice in your glory

I will remember the stories

Oh ancient of days

Mold me like clay

Show me which way is up

So we can sup fine dining

Am I whining

Is this my cry

Without asking why

I'll continue to try

Keep your servant humble

So that I don't stumble

Over my own feet

Make this path sweet

Clearly

Letting go only made me strong

I was able to see the wrong

Clearly I was able to see

Without anything blocking me

I am so thankful for the chances

Because of circumstances

We had to part

Now given another start

I am ready to begin

To follow this to the end

We're a work in progress

Let's not regress

Move forward

Towards higher heights

Like the Vegas lights

You shine bright

Like a diamond

You're cut to precision

My decision is to treat you like

The king you are you're truly a star

Stay close to me

Let's walk together let's talk together

Hate, envy lust belongs to the enemy.

He is lurking every step you make every breath you

Take he is there. He's in your head that's

Why it's so hard.

Just do the right reject all the wrong.

You are strong beautiful precious

Stones. Love is all we want and need

Love makes us all happy

Help a person, smile, share be kind.

The easy things are what we need

How can you have this much and

The next person don't have

How many cars can you drive?

How many houses can you live in?

How big can your diamonds be?

Wake up

You shine without all that.

You have style

You have your own thing

That makes everybody take notice.

We're a unique people

Our hair skin languages ideas

We are the best ever made

Jah loves us

The bible is real

Stop trying to be cause you already are

Stars

Blessed by the best.

Don't let anyone tell you otherwise

There is a war going on not over there

But here in your head that's where the war is.

The enemy is trying to get you on his side

Don't get confused you can still do everything

Just take out the negative

For real bad thoughts

belong to the enemy

We're all together striving to be as one

When you stray you get lost and confused

Stay with the masses. The masses are good

Don't think your going to get left out

Cause your not only if you want to

600k careless Ethiopians will go down

Don't be one of them.

You can be saved you just have to believe

Christ really died for us

You will get left with the rest

Who choose not to get their blessing

Do the right thing don't let your neighbor suffer

We are all watching each other

Don't get caught slipping

I believe watch me shine

Do you believe

It's not magic.

Change your heart and mind

Your soul will follow

That is what we are trying to save

The soul not the flesh

The flesh to be protected and taking care of

You are great special rare chosen`

Your precious

I can't find enough words

We must

Catch up we are far behind

But only in the mind

Material things are nothing

LISTEN TO THE MESSAGES

THEY ARE EVERYWHERE…

Knowledge is power

Know the ledge

So that you don't fall off the edge

If you have Wisdom

Wise the dumb

God made the dirt

If it hurts tell him to ease the pain

of getting to know his name.

Let's all be equal in our eyes

and

in our hearts for real

I'll be back

I have work to do

Let's all be safe

Gain knowledge

know who you are

Library books are free

Eventually

We will all BE

Stop competing with each other…

Shebah

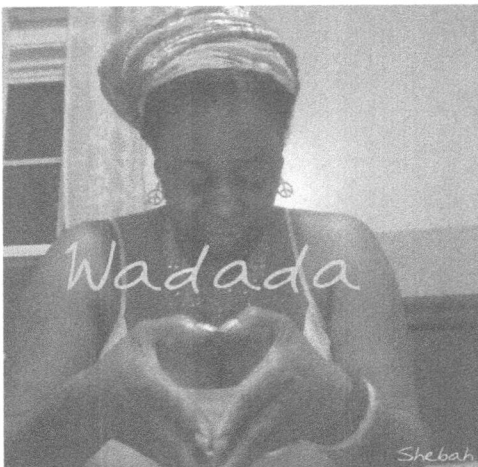

Shebah Ali a Teacher Poet and Author is currently a graduate student at NCCU. Born in Brooklyn NY, In early 1990 Shebah decided it was time for a change of scenery (and weather) and moved to Durham, NC. Shebah loves reaching others through her Prophetic Poetry. Shebah is a single mother of a teenage son who enjoys the outdoors and being in tune with nature.

Shebah Rising In The Judgement

ORDER FORM

*Name*_____

*Company*_____

*City*_____*State*___*Zip*____

*Day Phone*_____

*Evening Phone*_____

*E-Mail*_____

Cost: $12.99

Pleases make check or money order payable to:

The Gathering of the People

PO BOX 51231

Durham NC 27707-9998

Quantity of books $

Sub total $

NC residents Add 7% $

Shipping and handling $3.00 for first book

$.50 for each additional book $

Total Amount Due $

Shebahali@yaoo.com